what we do

CONTENTS

Words in **bold** appear in the glossary on page 24.

I AM A SHOP ASSISTANT

My name is Tilly. I work as a sales assistant in a fashion store in a shopping centre. This is the outside of the shop where I work (right).

My job is to sell **stock** to the customers. I assist the customers while they are shopping, handle payments and make sure the shop looks as attractive as possible.

The type of work a shop assistant carries out is similar in all kinds of shops. It doesn't matter if you are selling tools, books, furniture or electrical appliances, the important thing is to understand the products in your shop and help the customer find what they want.

KEY SKILLS

FRIENDLY AND OUTGOING – You need to interact and get on with many different types of customers, so you must have excellent people skills.

The most enjoyable part of my job is working as part of a team and making lots of sales. It is also satisfying to find clothes for the customers that make them look good. However, the work can be tiring as you spend long hours on your feet.

▼ *This is the view of our shop from behind the counter.*

WORKING CONDITIONS

Shop assistants spend a lot of their time moving around the shop floor, helping the customers and carrying stock. It can be hard work, especially when the shop gets very busy.

I work from 9.30am to 5.30pm, but some days the store stays open in the evening and I work longer hours.

KEY SKILLS

STAMINA – You must keep going and be pleasant and helpful to customers, even when you are tired and the shop is busy.

▼ *Welcoming the customers and asking if they need help is an important part of the job.*

The **shifts** a shop assistant works depend on the store, but you might have to be willing to work at weekends. There is often an increased rate of pay for working bank holidays, Sundays and overtime. Another benefit of the job is the staff **discount** you receive on all of the shop's products.

Each morning before the shop opens, our manager, Sanam, gets the team together for a staff **briefing** (below). She tells us the jobs that we need to do that day and shows us if we are meeting the shop's **sales targets**. We also talk about how we can increase sales. Sometimes we will create outfits, so that we have fashionable ideas to recommend to the customers.

▲ *I am constantly moving stock into position and checking that the rails look tidy.*

►*In the briefing, Sanam and the team look at why some products are selling and others are not.*

FINDING A JOB

▲ *A man looking for a job hands his CV to Sanam.*

WE NEED
YOU!

CHRISTMAS STAFF

we are looking for flexible
FULL and PART-TIME
Temporary Sales Advisors for Christmas

Previous experience within retail is essential.
If you're focused, ambitious and up for the challenge
of working with JOY throughout the Christmas period
we would love to hear from you.

Simply hand in your CV in store or email it to us
careers@joythestore.com

JOY
www.joythestore.com

If you fancy becoming a shop assistant there are plenty of stores, supermarkets and smaller shops in towns and cities that could be on the lookout for new staff. You do not need any special qualifications for the job, but shops often want people who have experience of working with the public.

Look out for job adverts online or in the local newspaper. Very often shops will have a notice in the window. It's a good idea to go into the shop and ask, even if they are not advertising. It helps if you have a knowledge of the types of products the shop is selling. Christmas is a good time to get into the industry as shops employ extra staff.

Basic training will happen on the job. Large stores often have a set training scheme that you follow. Here (above), I am showing Taslima, the new member of staff, how to use the till. I also explain to trainees how customers use the fitting rooms, and teach them how to greet the customers and make them feel comfortable.

► *Customers can only take a maximum of four pieces of clothing into a fitting room. We hang a numbered tag outside so we know how many items the customer should give back to us.*

▲ *Taslima practises using the* **scanner** *at the checkout.*

KEY SKILLS

TEAMWORK – It is important to work well as a team to keep the shop running smoothly.

CUSTOMER CARE

Looking after the customer is the main part of a shop assistant's job. You need to be friendly and helpful so the customers will come back and visit the shop again.

I stand on the shop floor ready to assist the customers if they need advice or guidance. When I talk to the customers I find out exactly what they are looking for and do everything I can to find them something suitable.

▶ *I will often go up to the customer and ask if they need help, especially if it looks like they need assistance or advice on what suits them.*

KEY SKILLS

ENTHUSIASM – You need to be energetic and willing to talk to customers all day. If you are friendly the customers will feel relaxed and comfortable in the shop.

When the customers try clothes on, they sometimes ask me for my advice. I check that the garment fits them properly and give my opinion on whether the style and colour suits them. It is important to be honest. I often tell the customer to try a different colour or size, or I suggest a different item of clothing that I think will look better.

▲ *I tell this customer that a belt would improve the shape and fit of the dress that she has just tried on.*

◀ *The customer in the fitting room asks for a different size so I hand it through to her.*

PRODUCT KNOWLEDGE

Shop assistants have to understand the products they are selling, so that they can help the customers and answer their questions. For example, they should know about the features, the quality and the availability of different products.

▶ *I help this customer choose a purse as a gift for her friend.*

KEY SKILLS

CONFIDENCE – When you give advice and information the customers will trust you if you sound confident.

In a sports shop, hardware store, or shop selling electrical items, such as computers, shop assistants need to give in-depth technical advice. Learning about the products will be part of your job training in any shop. In a clothes shop you need to have a keen sense of style and keep up to date with the latest fashions.

I know which kinds of clothes suit different body shapes so I can make recommendations to the customers. We want the customers to look good in the clothes we sell, so that other people will notice them and want to try out our shop for themselves.

I also advise the customers which clothes and **accessories** can be combined with each other. Here, I am showing a customer a pair of earrings which would go well with the dress she has chosen.

▼ *The earrings match with the bright feathery pattern on the dress.*

TAKING PAYMENTS

Serving customers behind the till and taking payments for their purchases is a major part of a shop assistant's job.

I scan the clothes the customer is buying, take the hangers off and unclip the **security tags** using a powerful magnet on the counter (below). Then I fold the clothes up neatly and carefully put them into a bag (above-right).

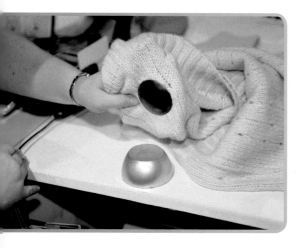

Shop assistants have to learn the different processes for handling various kinds of payment. If a customer pays in cash I key the amount into the till and give them the correct amount of change. When the customer pays with a **bank card** I operate a **chip and PIN** machine.

▲ *To make a payment straight from their bank account, the customer keys a secret code, called their PIN number, into the chip and PIN machine.*

If a customer has a gift voucher for the shop, they receive a discount on the price of the goods. Sometimes I pop a free voucher (below) into a customer's bag if I think they are a good customer who is likely to come back again.

At the end of each day I check that the cash, cheques and receipts from the card machine match with the amount of sales registered on the till (below).

KEY SKILLS

NUMERACY SKILLS – When you are dealing with money you need fast and accurate **mental arithmetic.**

DISPLAYING GOODS

Shop assistants constantly make sure that the shop is looking tidy and the shelves and rails are stocked in an attractive way.

Lola is in charge of the **merchandising** in our shop. She arranges the **mannequins** in our window display (below). **Head office** send us a picture of how they want the window to look, and deliver the props we need, but Lola changes the display slightly so it appeals to the customers in our local area.

▼ *Lola changes the window display every week.*

▲ *I arrange the necklaces neatly in the jewellery cabinet.*

Inside the shop we dress the mannequins to highlight our best-selling clothes. We also use the dummies to give the customers ideas of possible outfits and combinations. On the rails we often put eye-catching, expensive items at the front. New stock and clothes left in the fitting room are put on display as soon as possible. Here, Taslima is using a steamer to iron out the creases on a dress so it looks smart when it is on display (left).

It is important that the customers can clearly see if any goods are on sale or part of a special offer. We have a sale twice a year – once in the winter (below), and once in summer.

KEY SKILLS

PRESENTATION – It's important that you look good as well as the store. If you appear smart and stylish it gives the shop a positive image.

▶ *Lola clips the sale tags on so the customers can see which clothes are discounted.*

ORDERING STOCK

Shop assistants have to manage the levels of stock in the shop, and unpack and store new deliveries appropriately.

We receive a daily order from the **warehouse** to replace the goods we have sold. Every Monday I identify if there is any other stock I would like to add to the order. I check the storeroom (left) to see if we are short of anything and decide if there are any items we would like more of because they are selling well.

When the delivery arrives at the back of the shop our **security panel** beeps and a message flashes up telling us it can be collected.

▼ *Unpacking a delivery is quite exciting because new garments are sent to us all the time, especially at the start of a new season.*

▲ *The security panel also has an alarm for us to press if we spot anybody shoplifting. It alerts the security guards in the shopping centre.*

If the customer wants a piece of clothing, but we don't have the correct

ABILITY TO LEARN QUICKLY – You need to be good at learning procedures, such as placing an order, so that you don't make mistakes.

size in stock it usually means the warehouse has sold out. I can check on our computer system if any of our other shops around the country have it in stock. I can then ring that store (below) and arrange for it to be sent in the post to us.

AFTER-SALES

When we sell something over the counter we advise the customer of our returns **policy**. This tells them how they can return the item if they are not happy with it in any way.

If the customer decides their purchase does not suit them, they can exchange it for something else in the shop. First I look at their receipt to check it was bought in the last 14 days and then I check that the garment has been brought back in good condition.

▶ *When the customer returns an item they can exchange it or I issue them a **credit note** which they can use to buy something at a later date.*

JOY

Returns Policy

Whilst we do not offer a refund on unwanted items, we will offer an exchange or credit note on full price merchandise; if returned in saleable condition, with a receipt, within 14 days.

We do not offer exchange or credit notes on sale items.

This is in addition to your statutory rights.

JOY Head Office, 432 Coldharbour Lane, London SW9 8LG

Sometimes the customer will bring back an item that is faulty. On this woman's top the seam has split down the side (right). When this happens I ask the manager and ring head office to check that it is OK to refund the customer. Then I cross out the item on the customer's receipt and give them a refund in the same way that they paid. I make sure that I am apologetic and pleasant to unhappy customers.

Shop assistants sometimes have to deal with very angry customers. You have to keep calm, and be sensitive and understanding of the customer's feelings. Being patient and nice will usually sort out a difficult situation.

KEY SKILLS

POLITENESS –
Even with the most demanding customers you must show a polite and professional attitude.

GETTING ON

You do not necessarily need qualifications to work as a shop assistant, but training towards a *Certificate* or *Diploma in Retail Skills* could give your career a real boost.

■ The *Retail Skills* qualifications can be gained at *Levels 1, 2 and 3* and are awarded by bodies such as City & Guilds. They are available at the National Retail Skills Academy training centres and can also be taken at local colleges. There are also specialist qualifications, such as *Sales Professional and Visual Merchandising*. Big **retailers** often give you the chance to take these as part of your ongoing training.

KEY SKILLS

AMBITION – To advance your career you need the desire and drive to succeed.

▲ *Visual merchandisers present the goods in a shop in the best possible way.*

▶*Sanam, the store manager, makes the important decisions. Sometimes she decides the shop floor needs rearranging.*

■ It is very likely with experience and training that you will progress to more senior roles in the shop. I am now a supervisor, which means I assist Sanam our manager in directing and motivating the team. In a **chain store** like ours you can work your way up from store manager to area manager where you take charge of a number of shops.

■ Being a good sales assistant can help you on your way to other careers in retail, such as merchandising or buying. Buyers choose the goods that retail chains sell in their shops. Some shop assistants learn so much about the products that they decide to open their own shops. The choice is yours!

GLOSSARY

accessories Items or pieces of clothing that add style and colour to an outfit.

bank card A plastic card which allows customers to pay for goods directly from their bank account.

briefing A meeting for giving information or instructions.

chain store A group of shops owned by one firm and spread across the country.

chip and PIN A way of paying for goods with a bank card where you key in a PIN number. PIN stands for personal identification number.

credit note A note from the seller to the customer, which shows a sum of money that the customer can use to buy goods from the store.

CV Stands for curriculum vitae. It gives you details of a person's education, experience and qualifications.

discount A reduction on the normal price of a product.

head office The main office of a company, where important decisions are made.

mannequin A dummy used to display clothes in a shop.

mental arithmetic Counting and calculating sums in your head.

merchandising Displaying goods in a way that attracts the customers towards making a purchase.

policy A course of action decided by a business.

retailer A business that sells goods to people.

sales targets The amount of sales that the management of a store expects the shop to achieve.

scanner A device that reads the barcodes of goods and tells the shop assistant the price the customer has to pay.

security panel An electronic device with buttons that is used for raising the alarm and message alerts.

security tag A special tag fixed on a product so an alarm will be raised if that item is removed from the store without the customer paying for it.

shift A period of time in which you do your job.

stock A supply of goods kept in a shop and available to buy.

warehouse A large building where goods are stored before they are delivered to shops.

INDEX